Paul Gayler is executive chef at The Lanesborough in London, one of the most fabulous destination hotels in the world. He has worked in some of London's most prestigious restaurants, including The Dorchester and Inigo Jones. Paul has appeared on BBC2's *Saturday Kitchen* and Radio 4's *VegTalk*, as well as being a judge on ITV's *Chef of the Year*. His previous books for Kyle Cathie have been translated into 10 languages and sold 500,000 copies worldwide.

Paul Gayler's **little book of**
pasta & noodles

Paul Gayler's little book of
pasta & noodles

stunning, healthy, ready in minutes

Kyle Cathie Limited

contents

Fresh pasta is available from Italian delicatessens and high street supermarkets, but if you have time it is fun and tastier to make it at home. The basic dough is simple to make, and keeps for up to 3 days in the fridge or 1 month in the freezer.

home-made pasta

250g '00' pasta flour
pinch of salt
2 large beaten eggs
  plus 1 large beaten yolk
1 tablespoon olive oil
1 tablespoon water

making the dough

Sift the flour and salt on to a clean work surface, forming it into a mound, then make a well in the centre with your fingers. Pour the beaten eggs into the well, add the oil and water, then gradually mix the flour in towards the centre with your fingertips until all the ingredients have been combined into a paste.

Alternatively, put all the ingredients into a food processor and blend to mix for just a few seconds. Take care not to overwork the dough.

Gather the dough into a neat ball and knead for 4–5 minutes until it is smooth and pliable. Cover with clingfilm and leave to rest in the fridge for 1 hour.

rolling the dough

For lasagne sheets it is possible to roll out the pasta by hand with a rolling pin. Use a plain knife or plain pasta wheel to cut the dough into rectangles. For all other types of pasta, and to achieve a smoother lasagne, it is best to use a small hand-operated pasta machine.

Cut the rested pasta dough into 4–6 pieces. Put the pasta machine on setting no. 1 (the thickest setting), then feed a piece of dough through the rollers, which should be lightly floured to prevent the pasta sticking. Then put the machine on setting no. 2 and pass the dough through again. Continue in this way until the dough is very thin – maybe up to no. 4 or 5 setting. Repeat with each piece of dough.

cutting the dough

For spaghetti, linguine, fettuccine and other narrow ribbon shapes, simply attach the relevant noodle cutter to the pasta machine, and feed the pasta through.

For lasagne and cannelloni, cut the sheets of pasta into 10cm x 7.5cm rectangles. For pappardelle, cut the pasta into long ribbons 2.5cm wide.

To make ravioli, brush a sheet of pasta with water, and then place small teaspoonfuls of stuffing on it, about 5cm apart in rows. Cover with a second sheet of pasta, press down gently, then cut the pasta into squares with a pasta wheel or a sharp knife. Check the edges are well sealed. Ravioloni are made in the same way as ravioli but are slightly larger.

To make tortellini, cut the rolled-out pasta into circles with a 7.5cm plain cutter. Place a good teaspoonful of filling on one half of each circle, then brush the edges with a little water and fold in half, pressing gently to seal the edges together. Carefully fold each semi-circle around your finger to form a crescent shape.

variations

Black olive pasta

Purée, or very finely chop, 50g rinsed black olives and add to the flour at the same time as the eggs. No salt is necessary as the olives are already salty.

Grainy mustard pasta

Add 1 tablespoon of wholegrain mustard to the flour with the eggs.

Spiced pasta

Add ½ teaspoon ground spice – cumin, coriander, curry powder, saffron or even cinnamon – to the flour.

simple
yet delicious

Pasta and tomato sauce is a simple, delicious combination. The raw tomato sauce shown here can only be made during the summer when vine-ripened tomatoes are succulent and sweet-tasting. At other times, make the more traditional tomato sauce, with fresh or good-quality tinned tomatoes.

pasta & tomato sauce

raw tomato sauce
450g overripe vine plum tomatoes
    chopped
1 tablespoon tomato purée
10 basil leaves
1 tablespoon castor sugar
2 tablespoons sherry, or raspberry,
    vinegar
100ml olive oil
salt and freshly cracked black pepper

tomato sauce
15g unsalted butter
4 tablespoons olive oil
2 shallots, chopped
a sprig of thyme
1 small bay leaf
3 garlic cloves, crushed
1kg overripe vine plum tomatoes,
    deseeded and chopped (or 2 x 400g tins)
2 tablespoons tomato purée
1 tablespoon castor sugar
100ml tomato juice (optional)
salt and freshly cracked black pepper

500g fresh or 450g dried pasta of choice
freshly grated Parmesan cheese

raw tomato sauce

In a bowl, combine the tomatoes, purée, basil, sugar and vinegar. Cover and leave at room temperature for 2 hours.

Purée the mixture by putting it through a food mill (or blender) to form a smooth sauce. Whisk in the oil, and season to taste.

tomato sauce

Put the butter and oil in a pan and add the shallots, thyme, bay leaf and garlic. Sweat over a low heat until the shallots are softened and translucent.

Add the tomatoes, purée, sugar and tomato juice, if using. Bring to the boil, then reduce the heat and simmer, uncovered, for 20–25 minutes.

Use a ladle to press the sauce through a fine sieve. Season to taste.

Cook the pasta in a large pan of salted boiling water until al dente and drain thoroughly. Serve with tomato sauce of choice and freshly grated Parmesan cheese.

Bolognese sauce as a name doesn't actually exist in Italy, where it is just called a ragù. Tradition has it that the longer the sauce cooks, the better the flavour.

tagliatelle al ragù bolognese

for the ragù bolognese
50g unsalted butter
75g pancetta or smoked bacon, cut into small dice
1 onion, finely chopped
1 carrot, finely chopped
1 stick of celery, finely chopped
2 teaspoons chopped oregano
2 teaspoons thyme leaves
350g good quality lean minced beef
100g chicken livers, cleaned well and chopped
2 tablespoons tomato purée
100ml dry white wine
300ml beef stock
salt and freshly cracked black pepper
freshly grated nutmeg

500g fresh or 450g dried tagliatelle, fettucine or spaghetti
freshly grated Parmesan cheese

Melt the butter in a large, heavy based pan, add the pancetta and fry for 4–5 minutes, or until golden. Add the onion, carrot, celery and herbs and cook for a further 2 minutes. Stir in the minced beef, increase the heat and brown the meat well all over.

Add the chopped livers and cook for 2 minutes. Stir in the tomato purée and cook for 5 minutes. Add the wine and stock, then season lightly with salt, pepper and nutmeg. Bring to the boil, reduce to a low simmer and cook, covered, for at least 30 minutes.

Cook the tagliatelle in a large pan of salted boiling water until *al dente* and serve with the ragù and freshly grated Parmesan cheese.

One of the great Italian sauces, rich and extremely unctuous in flavour, carbonara does not traditionally contain any cream. Many cooks, however, feel that the addition of a little cream helps to stabilise the sauce. Although it is generally felt Parmesan is the preferred cheese, any Italian will tell you nothing other than pecorino will do!

pasta carbonara

2 tablespoons olive oil
125g salt pork or smoked bacon,
   cut into very small dice
1 garlic clove, crushed
3 free-range eggs, lightly beaten
2 tablespoons double cream
   (optional)
450g dried pasta
50g pecorino (or reggiano
   Parmesan) cheese, finely grated
salt and freshly cracked
   black pepper

Heat the oil in a pan, add the pork or bacon and cook until golden all over. Add the garlic and cook for 1 minute.

In a bowl, mix the eggs with the cream, if using.

Meanwhile, cook the pasta until just done, or *al dente*. Drain well, then add to the bacon and garlic pan. Pour over the eggs, or eggs and cream, quickly add the pecorino and toss to mix. Add salt and pepper to taste and serve immediately.

PG TIPS

Pecorino is a hard sheep's (ewe's) milk cheese made all over Italy, from the Italian word *pecora* meaning sheep. Most pecorino cheeses are aged and sharp in flavour, those from Rome (*romano*) and Sardinia (*sardo*) are the most commonly used and found outside Italy.

Here is my variation on the classic carbonara pasta, using dried wild mushrooms to replace the pork. These give a wonderfully earthy flavour, richness and aroma.

funghi carbonara

450g bucatini pasta (or spaghetti)
25g unsalted butter
20g dried wild mushrooms, soaked
    for 1 hour in water
1 shallot, finely chopped
150ml double cream
2 free-range eggs, beaten
100g grated Parmesan
salt, freshly ground black pepper and
    ground nutmeg

Cook the pasta in a large pan of boiling salted water until *al dente* and drain well.

Heat the butter in a large frying pan, add the mushrooms and shallot and sauté for 3–4 minutes until softened. Add the cream, bring to the boil and cook for 2–3 minutes or until the sauce has thickened slightly.

Add the pasta and stir in the beaten eggs and cheese. Toss well together and season with salt, pepper and nutmeg. Serve immediately.

PG TIPS
Mushrooms are a tasty healthy option, a good source of vitamins and other important minerals. Generally dried mushrooms have a much stronger flavour than fresh ones.

As a bit of a traditionalist, I make my pesto by using a mortar and pestle to pound the ingredients before adding the oil, but a blender does a quicker and equally successful job. The sauce will keep in the fridge for 2–3 days before losing its vibrant colour and freshness.

pasta al genovese

75g basil leaves
2 garlic cloves, chopped
1 tablespoon roughly chopped
    pine nuts
2 tablespoons finely grated
    Parmesan cheese
    (preferably reggiano)
100ml extra virgin olive oil
salt and freshly cracked
    black pepper

450g dried pasta

For the pesto sauce, put the basil, garlic, pine nuts and Parmesan in a blender. With the motor running, slowly pour in the oil in a thin stream through the feeder tube, and process until smooth. Add salt and pepper to taste, transfer to a bowl (or container with a lid), cover and refrigerate until needed.

Cook the pasta in boiling salted water until *al dente* and drain thoroughly. Stir in the pesto sauce, or serve it separately if preferred.

PG TIPS
You can replace the basil with another favourite herb: flat leaf parsley, coriander or mint for example, or use rocket leaves for a hotter taste. Cooked asparagus spears or broccoli heads make interesting alternative tastes. You can also replace the pine nuts with hazlenuts, or with lightly roasted pumpkin seeds, or use soft goat's cheese instead of the Parmesan.

rigatoni & mixed peppers

with coriander & goat's cheese pesto

for the pesto
1 garlic clove, crushed
50g fresh coriander leaves
1 tablespoon pine kernels
150ml extra virgin olive oil
2 tablespoons freshly grated
   Parmesan
75g soft mild goat's cheese
50g mascarpone
salt and freshly ground black
   pepper

4 peppers (1 red, 1 green, 1 yellow,
   1 orange)
50g unsalted butter
2 tablespoons olive oil
pinch of sugar
450g rigatoni
salt and freshly ground black
   pepper
fresh coriander leaves, to garnish
   (optional)

For the pesto, blitz the garlic, coriander and pine kernels to a purée in a blender, gradually adding the olive oil. Add the cheeses and blend again. Season.

Halve and deseed the peppers, then cut them into strips 5mm wide. Heat the butter and oil in a frying pan, add the pepper strips and cook gently for 10–15 minutes. If they begin to stick to the pan, add a little water. When the peppers are tender, stir in the sugar and some salt and pepper to taste.

Cook the rigatoni in a large pan of boiling salted water until *al dente*, then drain well. Stir the pasta into the peppers, add the pesto sauce and lightly toss together. Adjust the seasoning, garnish with coriander leaves if liked, and serve straight away.

PG TIPS

For a really quick sauce, use bottled peppers in oil, and for a little variation why not try adding a few sautéed bacon lardons to the cooked pasta? Any other shaped pasta would look pretty in this dish.

The Chinese black beans called for in this recipe are soya beans that have been fermented and salted. They are soft and slightly pulpy and are usually chopped to release their pungent flavour. Don't confuse them with black beans or turtle beans used in South American cooking.

hot aubergine pasta

with Chinese black beans & peanut butter sauce

500g fresh or 450g dried penne pasta
4 tablespoons vegetable or sunflower oil
1 tablespoon sesame oil
1 aubergine, cut into 1cm dice
2.5cm piece of root ginger, peeled and finely chopped
1 garlic clove
2 tablespoons dried Chinese black beans, chopped
1 small green chilli, deseeded and finely chopped
1 tablespoon sugar
2 tablespoons hoisin sauce
1 tablespoon smooth peanut butter
3 spring onions, finely chopped
2 tablespoons chopped fresh coriander

Cook the penne in a large pan of boiling salted water until *al dente* and drain well.

Heat both oils in a wok or large frying pan, add the diced aubergine, ginger and garlic and stir fry over a low heat for 2–3 minutes. Add the black beans and green chilli and stir for a further 2 minutes. Add the sugar, hoisin sauce and peanut butter and cook until reduced and thickened.

Add the pasta to the sauce and then the spring onions and coriander. Stir until heated through and serve immediately.

tagliatelle with caramelised chicory

& deep-fried lemon zest

3 lemons
4 heads of white chicory (endive)
50g unsalted butter
1 teaspoon sugar
salt and freshly ground black pepper
50g raisins, soaked in hot water
  for 30 minutes and drained
100ml double cream
500g fresh or 450g dried tagliatelle
  pasta
50g freshly grated Parmesan
100ml vegetable oil

Zest the lemons and place the zest into a small bowl. Halve the lemons and squeeze the juice over the zest, leave for 20 minutes to marinate and accentuate the flavour.

Remove and discard any tough outer leaves from the chicory. Trim the root ends, then halve the chicory lengthways and shred crossways into strips. Set aside. Melt the butter in a pan, add the chicory, sugar, a little salt and pepper and sauté over a moderate heat for about 15 minutes, stirring occasionally, until the chicory is golden and caramelised. Add the raisins and cream. Remove the lemon zest from the juice, dry in a cloth and add the juice to the chicory. Simmer for about 1–2 minutes until the sauce thickens. Keep warm.

Cook the tagliatelle in a large pan of boiling salted water for 2–3 minutes or until *al dente*, then drain, reserving 100ml cooking water. Add the water to the lemon cream. Toss the sauce with the pasta and half the cheese and season to taste.

Heat the vegetable oil in a small pan, add the lemon zest and fry for about 1 minute until lightly golden and crisp. Drain on kitchen paper. Serve the pasta in 4 bowls, sprinkle over the remaining cheese and scatter over the crispy fried lemon.

Bigoli is a thick wholewheat spaghetti from Venice, usually served with robust sauces such as anchovy and onion, or this spicy mixture of minced pork and chicken livers. If you can't find bigoli, bucatini makes a good substitute.

bigoli

with spicy meat sauce

350g minced pork
salt and freshly ground black pepper
6 tablespoons olive oil
1 onion, finely chopped
1 carrot, finely chopped
1 celery stick, finely chopped
1 garlic clove, finely chopped
1 teaspoon dried red chilli flakes
100g chicken livers, cleaned and
  finely diced
150ml red wine
2 tablespoons tomato purée
150ml tomato passata
pinch of sugar
450g bigoli pasta
grated nutmeg
1 tablespoon chopped sage

Season the pork with salt and pepper. Heat 4 tablespoons of the oil in a heavy based frying pan, then add the pork and cook over a high heat until sealed all over. Stir in the vegetables, garlic and chilli flakes and cook for 2–3 minutes. Add the diced chicken livers, cover the pan and cook for 5 minutes, then pour in the red wine, cover again and cook for 2 minutes longer. Stir in the tomato purée, passata, sugar and a little salt, then reduce the heat, cover and cook for about 20–30 minutes, stirring occasionally.

Cook the pasta in plenty of boiling salted water until *al dente*, then drain well. Toss the pasta with the remaining oil and some grated nutmeg, salt and pepper. Add the meat sauce and chopped sage, toss together, then serve.

A great and simple dish using sheep's cheese. Try adding crisply fried, diced pancetta to the pasta.

tagliatelle with capers

fried egg & pecorino sardo

500g tagliatelle
freshly grated nutmeg
salt and freshly ground black
  pepper
40g unsalted butter
2 tablespoons superfine capers,
  rinsed and drained
4 free-range eggs
a little clarified butter (see
  PG TIPS)
100g pecorino sardo (or Parmesan),
  cut into shavings
freshly cracked black pepper (see
  PG TIPS)

Cook the pasta in boiling salted water until *al dente*, then drain well and return to the pan. Season with nutmeg, salt and pepper. Add the butter and capers and toss together well. Keep warm.

Quickly fry the eggs in clarified butter and season with salt. Arrange the pasta on warmed serving plates, top each portion with a fried egg and scatter over the pecorino shavings. Sprinkle with a little freshly cracked black pepper and serve.

PG TIPS

To clarify butter, heat gently in a small pan until it begins to boil. Boil for 2 minutes, then pour off through a fine conical strainer or a muslin-lined sieve, leaving the white, milky sediment in the pan. Store in the fridge.

To make cracked black pepper, pound peppercorns roughly in a pestle and mortar.

porcini
pappardelle

with grilled figs

for the porcini pappardelle
25g dried porcini mushrooms
2 garlic cloves, crushed
3 tablespoons extra virgin olive oil
450g '00' pasta flour
3 free-range eggs

3 tablespoons olive oil
175g fresh porcini (or 50g soaked
  and dried)
1 small mild red chilli, deseeded
  and finely chopped
6 firm but ripe purple figs,
  cut into wedges
½ teaspoon castor sugar
2 tablespoons balsamic vinegar
50g freshly grated Parmesan
juice of ½ lemon
salt, freshly ground black pepper
  and ground nutmeg

For the pasta, soak the mushrooms in warm water for 20 minutes, reserving the soaking liquid. Rinse well, chop finely and mix with the garlic and oil. Sift the flour into a bowl, add the mushroom mixture and eggs, and mix together. Knead for 10–12 minutes until smooth and elastic. Wrap in clingfilm and leave to rest for 1 hour. Divide the dough into 4, then, working 1 piece at a time, roll it out until paper thin. Sprinkle with a little flour, then roll up. Cut the roll widthways into 2cm wide ribbons. Unroll the ribbons and lay out on a lightly floured tray. Leave to dry for 30 minutes.

Preheat a grill to its highest setting. Heat a frying pan with 1½ tablespoons of olive oil, add the porcini and chilli and cook until the mushrooms are golden. Dust the figs with a little sugar, put on a baking sheet, place under the grill and cook until lightly caramelised.

Bring the reserved mushroom liquid and 1.5 litres of water to the boil in a large pan. Cook the pasta for 3 minutes, drain and add to the mushrooms. Stir in the vinegar and cheese. Add the lemon juice, season and arrange on serving plates. Top with caramelised fig wedges and drizzle over the remaining olive oil.

For me Brie served in any way is a real treat, wonderfully creamy, a great partner for the buttery pasta.

tagliatelle with creamy brie

& sunblush tomatoes

25g unsalted butter
1 shallot, finely chopped
½ garlic clove, crushed
1 teapoon fresh thyme leaves
200g sunblush tomatoes in oil,
   drained
500g fresh or 450g dried tagliatelle
100ml crème fraîche
   or double cream
150g brie, rind removed, sliced
salt and freshly ground black
   pepper

Melt the butter in a pan, add the shallot and garlic and cook over a low heat for 5 minutes. Add the thyme and tomatoes, increase the heat and cook for about 2 minutes until softened.

Cook the tagliatelle in boiling salted water until *al dente* and drain well. Add the crème fraîche and brie to the tomatoes and stir until melted. Return the pasta to the pan, pour over the sauce and toss together. Season to taste and serve.

PG TIPS
Use a combination of different colours and flavours of tagliatelle in this dish, such as tomato, mushroom and spinach.

Although I have used bucatini pasta for this recipe, other pastas such as linguini and fettucine are equally suitable. Whenever I make this simple dish at home it transports me to the Greek islands in a instant. Hot pickled chillies are available from Middle Eastern delicatessens.

bucatini with feta & pickled chilli

tomato & mint

4 tablespoons good quality olive oil
1 small garlic clove, crushed
3 tablespoons chopped fresh mint
4 ripe but firm plum tomatoes cut into ½cm dice
300g Greek feta, cut into small ½cm dice
450g bucatini
salt
2 small hot pickled chillies, finely chopped

Heat half the oil in a large frying pan over a medium heat, add the garlic and cook for 1 minute until it becomes translucent. Stir in the mint, add the chopped tomatoes and diced feta and cook for a further 2–3 minutes.

Meanwhile, cook the bucatini in a large pan of boiling salted water until *al dente*. Drain the pasta in a colander and add to the pan. Add the chopped pickled chillies and toss the mixture together.

Divide the pasta between 4 serving pasta bowls and drizzle over the remaining oil.

summer vegetable tagliatelle

with lemon & tarragon

for the lemon dressing
juice of ½ lemon
1 tablespoon olive oil
1 teaspoon honey
2 spring onions, finely chopped
2 tablespoons roughly chopped
  tarragon

200g asparagus
100g baby courgettes, cut into thick
  slices
50g fresh or frozen peas
500g fresh or 450g dried tagliatelle
12 sunblush tomatoes
freshly ground black pepper

Prepare a light lemon dressing by whisking together in a bowl the lemon juice, olive oil, honey, spring onions and tarragon.

Break off the woody end stems of the asparagus and, using a potato peeler, carefully peel the tips. Cut into 2.5cm lengths. Cook for 2 minutes in boiling water, then remove with a slotted spoon and quickly refresh in cold water. Cook the courgettes in the boiling water for 1 minute, remove and quickly refresh in cold water. Add the peas to the boiling water and cook for 2–3 minutes, remove and quickly refresh.

Cook the fresh pasta in plenty of boiling water for 2–3 minutes until *al dente* (dried pasta will need a little longer). Drain the pasta, reserving 65ml of the cooking water, then return the pasta to the pan, add the drained asparagus, courgettes and peas with the tomatoes and toss well. Add the lemon dressing and reserved pasta water, season with black pepper to taste, toss well together and serve.

baked & filled dishes

rolled butternut squash lasagne

with wild garlic & pesto cream

400g butternut squash (or pumpkin),
  peeled, deseeded and cut into
  large pieces
6 tablespoons olive oil
3 tablespoons chopped fresh
  wild garlic
200g ricotta, well drained
1 tablespoon double cream
4 tablespoons fresh white
  breadcrumbs
1 quantity of pasta dough (see
  page 6), made into 12 fresh
  lasagne sheets
2 tablespoons freshly grated
  Parmesan
salt and freshly ground black pepper

for the pesto cream
45g fresh flat leaf parsley
2 tablespoons chopped fresh
  rosemary leaves
2 garlic cloves
45g blanched almonds
2 tablespoons olive oil
25g freshly grated Parmesan
25g unsalted butter
25g plain flour
300ml whole or soy milk
4 tablespoons double cream
salt and freshly ground black pepper

Preheat the oven to 190°C/375°F/gas mark 5. Put the squash in a roasting tin, drizzle over the olive oil and cook for 25 minutes until the flesh is tender. Remove and leave to cool. Reduce the oven to 150°C/300°F/gas mark 2.

For the pesto cream, place the herbs, garlic, almonds and olive oil in a blender and blitz to a coarse paste. Stir in the Parmesan. Melt the butter in a pan, stir in the flour, cook for 1–2 minutes, then add the milk and bring to the boil. Stir constantly with a whisk, reduce the heat and simmer for 2–3 minutes until thickened, smooth and glossy. Add the cream and the pesto and stir well. Season to taste.

In a bowl, mix the wild garlic, ricotta, cream, squash and breadcrumbs and season to taste.

Cook the lasagne sheets in boiling water until *al dente*, then transfer to cold water. Drain and pat the sheets dry with a cloth. Divide the squash mixture equally between the lasagne sheets, ensuring it covers them completely. Roll up like a Swiss roll, starting from one short end. Lightly grease a suitable ovenproof dish, then arrange the filled lasagne rolls in it. Pour the pesto sauce over the rolls, ensuring they are completely covered. Scatter over the Parmesan, then bake for 15–20 minutes until the top is golden and slightly crusty.

potato & greens cannelloni

with white bean & rosemary ragoût

for the ragoût
400g haricot beans, soaked
    overnight and drained
4 tablespoons olive oil
1 small onion, finely chopped
1 carrot, cut into small dice
2 garlic cloves, crushed
pinch of red chilli flakes
1 tablespoon chopped
    fresh rosemary
100ml dry white wine
200g sunblush tomatoes, chopped

600g new potatoes, scrubbed
2 tablespoons mild olive oil
2 garlic cloves, crushed
50g rocket leaves, stems trimmed
50g watercress leaves
175g dolcelatte cheese
12 fresh lasagne sheets (see page 6)
100ml pesto sauce (see page 18)
salt, freshly ground black pepper
    and ground nutmeg

For the ragoût, place the beans in a large pan, cover with cold water, bring to the boil, then simmer for 1–1½ hours until the beans are tender, adding more water if needed. Drain the beans, reserving their cooking liquid.

Heat half the olive oil in a pan, add the onion, carrot, garlic, chilli flakes and rosemary and cook for 3–4 minutes. Add the white wine and boil for 2 minutes. Add the beans and 150ml of their cooking liquid to the pan along with the tomatoes. Cook for a further 5 minutes, then stir in the remaining olive oil and season to taste.

Cook the new potatoes in boiling salted water for about 20 minutes until tender and then drain. Heat the olive oil in a pan, add the garlic, rocket and watercress and cook for 1 minute until wilted. Add the potatoes and lightly crush them together. Transfer to a bowl to cool. Mix with the dolcelatte and season to taste.

Cook the lasagne sheets in boiling water until *al dente*, then transfer to cold water. Drain and pat dry with a cloth, then season. Fill with the potato mixture, roll up and brush with olive oil. Reheat in a hot oven. Warm the bean ragoût, divide between 4 serving bowls, top each with three cannelloni, and top with pesto sauce.

Fresh peas are obviously a lot more work for the preparation of these ravioli, but really do make a difference. This dish always makes an appearance on my menu when the first peas come into season in spring.

green pea ravioli

with saffron & truffled beetroot salad

for the green pea ravioli
300g fresh shelled peas (or frozen)
20g fresh mint leaves
100g good quality ricotta cheese,
2 spring onions, finely chopped
1 tablespoon lemon juice
1 quantity pasta dough (see
    page 6)
salt and freshly ground black pepper

for the saffron butter sauce
150ml good vegetable stock
100ml double cream
good pinch of good quality saffron
40g unsalted butter, chilled and cut
    into small pieces
salt and freshly ground black pepper

for the truffled beetroot salad
1 tablespoon balsamic vinegar
pinch of sugar
½ tablespoon truffle oil
1 medium-sized beetroot, cooked,
    peeled and cut into
    julienne strips
1 truffle, cut into julienne strips
    (optional)
50g pea shoots

For the ravioli, cook the peas in boiling water for 5–6 minutes then drain (reserving 100ml of the cooking water). Refresh in iced water, drain again and dry well. Blend in a food processor with the mint, ricotta and spring onions to a coarse purée. Remove to a bowl, season and add the lemon juice. Roll out the pasta into thin sheets, then brush a sheet with water and place tablespoons of the pea-ricotta mixture on it, about 5cm apart in rows. Cover with a second sheet of pasta, press down gently, then cut into squares with a pasta wheel or sharp knife. Check the edges are well sealed, place on a lightly floured tray and leave to dry for 20 minutes.

For the saffron butter, heat the vegetable stock, reserved pea liquid, cream and saffron in a pan and simmer until it has reduced by half. Remove from the heat, whisk in the chilled butter, season to taste and then strain through a fine strainer.

Cook the ravioli in simmering salted water for 3–4 minutes, then remove and drain well. Whisk together the vinegar, sugar and oil, add the beetroot and fresh truffle and mix well. Divide the ravioli between 4 serving dishes, pour over the sauce, top with the beetroot salad and pea shoots and serve.

topfenravioli

with *prosciutto* & spinach

1 quantity pasta dough (see
  page 6)
75g unsalted butter
450g young spinach leaves
100g cottage cheese, well drained
75g *prosciutto*, finely diced
50g buffalo or cow's milk
  mozzarella, finely diced
2 tablespoons freshly grated
  Parmesan, plus extra to serve
10 fresh basil leaves, roughly
  chopped, plus a few whole
  leaves to garnish
salt and freshly ground black
  pepper
freshly grated nutmeg

First make the pasta dough. Cover with cling film and
leave to rest at room temperature for 15–30 minutes.

Meanwhile, make the filling. Heat 25g of the butter in
a large pan, add the spinach and cook for just a few
minutes, until it has wilted and all the excess moisture
has evaporated. Transfer to a bowl and leave to cool,
then chop finely. Stir in the cottage cheese, prosciutto,
mozzarella, Parmesan and chopped basil. Season to
taste with nutmeg, salt and pepper.

Roll out the dough using a pasta machine if you have
one. Alternatively, divide it into 2 batches and roll it out
very thinly by hand. It should be so thin that it is almost
translucent. Lightly brush 1 sheet of the dough with
water, then put teaspoonfuls of stuffing on it about 5cm
apart, in rows. Cover with the second sheet of pasta,
press down gently, then cut round the stuffing with a
round 6cm fluted pastry cutter. Check that the edges of
the ravioli are well sealed.

Cook the ravioli in gently simmering salted water for
2–3 minutes, until *al dente*, then drain well. Heat the
remaining butter in a frying pan until it is foaming,
golden brown and smells nutty (the bottom of the pan
will be covered with brown butter specks). Drizzle the
butter over the ravioli and sprinkle with more freshly
grated Parmesan and a few basil leaves before serving.

baked macaroni & Jerusalem artichoke soufflé

with Gruyère fondue

275g Jerusalem artichokes (or celeriac), peeled and cut into large dice
200g macaroni (or sedani) pasta
salt, freshly ground black pepper and ground nutmeg
45g unsalted butter
45g plain flour
600ml milk
5 free-range egg yolks
150g Roquefort cheese, crumbled
6 free-range egg whites
600ml double cream
200g finely grated Gruyère cheese

4 x 8cm diameter tartlet moulds or soufflé dishes

Simmer the Jerusalem artichokes in a pan of boiling water for 18–20 minutes. Drain and mash until smooth. Cook the macaroni in a large pan of boiling salted water until *al dente*. Season with salt, pepper and nutmeg.

Preheat the oven to 200°C/400°F/gas mark 6. Melt the butter in a heavy-based pan, add the flour and cook over a low heat for 1 minute. Add the milk, whisk until smooth, and cook for a further 3–4 minutes. Remove from the heat and cool slightly before beating in the egg yolks. Stir in the Roquefort and artichokes. Keep warm.

Whisk the egg whites until firm. Add one third of the whisked whites to the artichoke mixture, then gently fold in the remainder. Finally fold in the cooked pasta, then spoon into 4 well-buttered tartlet moulds. Place them in the oven for 3 minutes only, until the top of each soufflé begins to turn golden. Remove and turn out the soufflés into individual gratin dishes.

Heat the double cream over a moderate heat and stir in the Gruyère. Pour the fondue over the soufflés, then bake for a further 5 minutes before serving immediately.

Smoked haddock is a great fish, very flavourful and fairly inexpensive. Always buy natural smoked haddock rather than the yellow dyed variety, which is more readily available. This is real comfort food, but without the calories.

baked smoked haddock pasta

4 rashers lean smoked bacon
300g bucatini pasta
200ml skimmed milk
350g smoked haddock fillet, skinned
1 egg yolk
2 egg whites
3 tablespoons crème fraîche
2 tablespoons Cheddar cheese
2 teaspoons Dijon mustard
freshly ground black pepper

Preheat the oven to 190°C/375°F/gas mark 5. Place the bacon rashers on a non-stick baking tray and cook for 10 minutes until lightly crisp, remove and roughly chop into pieces. Cook the pasta in boiling water until *al dente* and drain well.

In a pan, bring the milk to the boil. Lower the heat, add the smoked haddock and poach for 3–4 minutes. Remove the fish with a slotted spoon and, when cool, lightly flake it, then strain the milk.

Pour the cooking milk into a bowl, and allow to cool slightly. Add the eggs, crème fraîche, half the Cheddar and the mustard, then season to taste with black pepper. Add the fish and bacon to the cream mix and combine well together.

Place the bucatini in an ovenproof baking dish, pour over the smoked haddock and bacon cream, toss together and scatter over the remaining Cheddar. Bake for 20–25 minutes until set and the top is bubbling and golden.

A simple but wonderfully intense dish, this recipe is one of my great favourites when I feel like something tasty and comforting.

tuscan baked chicken

450g chicken breasts, skinless and boneless
2 garlic cloves, peeled, thinly sliced
1 tablespoon fresh oregano, chopped
salt and freshly ground black pepper
2 tablespoons olive oil
200g tinned tomatoes, drained and chopped
250g fresh tomatoes, diced
1 teaspoon sugar
50g stoned black olives
150ml dry white wine
350g penne pasta
1 tablespoon superfine capers, rinsed
freshly grated reggiano Parmesan
30ml vegetable stock

Cut the chicken into bite-sized pieces and place in a dish. Add the garlic, ½ tablespoon oregano, salt and pepper, cover with clingfilm, and chill for 3 hours.

Preheat the oven to 180°C/350°F/gas mark 4. Heat the olive oil in a frying pan. Add the chicken and brown all over, then remove from pan. Add the tinned and fresh tomatoes to the pan, along with the sugar, olives and white wine, and simmer for 5 minutes.

Cook the pasta in boiling water, until *al dente*, then remove and drain. Add to the tomato sauce along with the capers, remaining oregano and season to taste. Finally add the chicken and toss well.

Transfer to a baking dish, sprinkle over the Parmesan cheese and place in the oven for 10–12 minutes until the cheese is golden and bubbling. Allow to cool slightly before serving.

PG TIPS
Try replacing the chicken with rabbit or seafood for a delicious variation.

pumpkin cappelletti

with pumpkin crisps

for the cappelletti
400g piece of pumpkin (or
  butternut squash), peeled,
  deseeded and cut into large
  chunks
1 tablespoon mild olive oil
½ teaspoon fennel seeds, lightly
  crushed
1 free-range egg yolk
2 amaretti biscuits, crushed
25g fresh white breadcrumbs
½ teaspoon Thai red curry paste
2 tablespoons mango chutney,
  finely chopped
salt, freshly ground black pepper
  and ground nutmeg

24 wonton wrappers

for the pumpkin crisps
150g wedge of pumpkin, peeled
vegetable oil, for deep-frying

for the curried carrot cream
2 carrots, cut into small dice
150ml good vegetable stock
1 teaspoon Thai red curry paste
6 tablespoons double cream
15g unsalted butter
few fresh coriander leaves,
  chopped

Preheat the oven to 200°C/400°F/gas mark 6. Sprinkle the pumpkin with oil and fennel seeds, then roast for 25 minutes, turning occasionally. Once cool, crush in a bowl with a fork. Mix in the remaining filling ingredients and refrigerate.

For the crisps, pare long thin strips off the pumpkin, then deep-fry in hot (150°C/300°F) vegetable oil, four or five strips at a time until golden and crisp. Drain on kitchen paper.

Lay out the wonton wrappers on a flat surface, place ½ tablespoon of filling in each square. Brush each square with a little water and fold over on the diagonal. Press the sides to seal. Hold one corner on the long side between thumb and index finger. Wrap around and press the two corners together. Place on a lightly floured tray and leave to dry for 30 minutes.

For the curried carrot cream, cook the carrot in the vegetable stock and curry paste for 10 minutes. Blend to a purée, then add the cream and butter and bring to the boil. Season to taste, add some coriander and keep warm.

Cook the cappelletti in a large pan of boiling salted water for 3–4 minutes, then remove and drain well. Season and then toss with the curried carrot cream. Place on 4 serving plates, top with the pumpkin crisps and serve.

plum tomato tortellini

with courgettes in a garlic broth

for the tortellini
3 tablespoons extra virgin olive oil
1.5kg firm, ripe plum tomatoes,
    skinned, halved and deseeded
1 clove garlic, crushed
½ teaspoon sugar
6 basil leaves, freshly chopped
salt and freshly ground black
    pepper
1 quantity basic pasta dough
    (see page 6)
freshly grated nutmeg

for the broth
4 large cloves garlic, peeled
    and halved
300ml chicken or vegetable stock
50g unsalted butter
2 courgettes, finely shredded

Heat the oil in a pan, add the tomatoes and cook gently for 1 minute, until softened. Add the garlic and sugar and continue to cook over a low heat for 10 minutes, until the tomatoes become slightly caramelised. Transfer to a bowl and leave to cool. Drain the tomatoes of excess juice if necessary, then chop them roughly and stir in the basil. Add salt and pepper to taste.

Roll out the pasta and cut into circles with a 7.5cm plain cutter. Place a good teaspoon of the tomato filling on one half of each circle, then brush the edges with a little water and fold in half, pressing gently to seal the edges together. Carefully fold each semi-circle around your finger to form a crescent shape. Refrigerate.

For the garlic broth, put the garlic cloves and stock into a pan, bring to the boil, then lower the heat and simmer gently for 30 minutes or until the stock has reduced by half its original volume. Strain, then whisk in the butter a piece at a time to make a light, buttery broth. Adjust the seasoning, then stir in the shredded courgettes.

Cook the tortellini in gently simmering water until *al dente*, then drain and season with nutmeg, salt and pepper. Divide the pasta between warmed serving bowls, coat with the garlic broth and serve immediately.

orecchiette

with chickpeas, broccoli, garlic, basil & olive oil

for the orecchiette
200g '00' pasta flour
100g durum wheat semolina
salt
2 tablespoons olive oil
200ml warm water

for the sauce
300g broccoli (or tenderstem
   broccoli, or any kind of greens)
4 tablespoons extra-virgin olive oil
2 garlic cloves, crushed
1 red onion, halved
   and thinly sliced
pinch of red chilli flakes
200g cooked chickpeas (tinned are
   fine), drained
10 fresh basil leaves, torn in pieces
6 fresh mint leaves, torn in pieces
freshly grated Parmesan cheese
   (optional)
salt and freshly ground black
   pepper

For the orecchiette, mix together the flour and semolina and make a well in the centre. Add a pinch of salt, the olive oil and water. Work in the flour from the edges and knead the dough for at least 10 minutes, then place in a lightly floured bowl, cover with a tea towel and leave to stand for 30 minutes. Divide the dough into 4 and roll into long strips 1cm in diameter, then cut each roll into 1cm pieces and roll these into balls. Flatten each ball with the thumb so that the dough resembles a 'little ear'. Place on a floured tea towel, cover and leave to dry for a few hours.

For the sauce, cut the broccoli into small florets and the stalk into large pieces. Cook in plenty of boiling salted water for 4–5 minutes – it should be fairly well cooked. Remove and drain in a colander.

Cook the orecchiette in a large pan of boiling salted water for about 4–5 minutes, remove and drain.

Heat the olive oil in a large frying pan, add the garlic, onion and chilli flakes and cook over a low heat for 4–5 minutes or until the onion is tender. Add the orecchiette, cooked broccoli and chickpeas and gently toss together. Scatter over the herbs, season to taste and serve. Serve the grated cheese separately if preferred.

elegant entertaining

These tiny venus clams are extremely sweet and tender, wonderful served raw with nothing more than a squeeze of lemon juice.

bucatini

with clams, garlic & chorizo

48 baby venus clams
450g bucatini pasta
6 tablespoons olive oil
2 garlic cloves, crushed
1 tablespoon finely chopped flat leaf
  parsley
5 tablespoons dry white wine
400g can tomatoes, chopped
½ teaspoon finely chopped dried
  peperoncino chilli
75g chorizo, outer casing removed,
  cut into 5mm dice

Scrub the clams under cold running water, discarding any open ones that don't close when tapped on a work surface. Set aside.

Cook the pasta in a large pan of boiling salted water until *al dente*.

Meanwhile, heat half the oil in a large pan over a medium heat, add the garlic and cook for 1 minute without letting it colour. Stir in the parsley, then add the clams and pour over the white wine. Cover with a lid and leave to steam for 2 minutes. Add the tomatoes, chilli and chorizo and pour over the remaining olive oil. Cover again and leave to cook for a further 2 minutes, until the clams open.

Drain the pasta. Stir the clam and chorizo sauce, then toss together with the pasta and serve immediately in individual bowls.

PG TIPS
Any type of clam is suitable for this dish; mussels would also be good.

In this recipe the ravioli filling is detached from its pasta casing, which is served alongside in the form of macaroni. These are the lightest of spinach dumplings imaginable, topped with a deliciously spicy dressing.

spinach ravioli

with macaroni & vegetable arrabiata dressing

350g fresh spinach, washed and
  stalks removed
190g good quality ricotta cheese,
  well drained
1 free-range egg
300g plain flour
40g freshly grated Parmesan
200g macaroni pasta (1cm thick)
salt, freshly ground black pepper
  and nutmeg

for the vegetable arrabiata dressing
100ml olive oil
2 shallots, finely chopped
2 garlic cloves, crushed
2 small dried red chillies,
  finely chopped
1 large courgette, finely diced
6 tomatoes, blanched, skinned,
  deseeded and chopped
2 tablespoons stoned, chopped black
  olives
juice of ½ lemon
50g chopped fresh coriander
salt and freshly ground black pepper

Cook the spinach until wilted in its own juices. Squeeze out any excess liquid, blitz to a purée, and transfer to a bowl. Add the ricotta, egg, flour and Parmesan, season and stir. Cover with clingfilm and refrigerate for 1 hour.

For the dressing, heat the olive oil in a pan, add the shallots, garlic and chillies and cook over a moderate heat for 30 seconds. Raise the heat, add the courgette and fry for 2 minutes. Add the tomatoes and olives and cook for a further 2–3 minutes. Add the lemon juice and coriander and season to taste. Keep warm.

To make the dumplings, use floured hands to roll the spinach mix into small 1cm balls. Bring a large pan of salted water to the boil, then carefully drop the dumplings into the water. When they rise to the surface (after a few minutes), remove them with a slotted spoon and drain well. Meanwhile, cook the macaroni in a large pan of boiling salted water until *al dente*. Toss the dumplings and pasta in the dressing, season to taste and divide between 4 serving bowls.

Orzo is a rice-shaped pasta, used here instead of rice to make a sort of risotto – or orzotto. If you can find chilli pecorino, sustitute it for pecorino, but reduce the jalapeño quantity.

shiitake & butternut squash orzotto

with chilli pecorino

2 tablespoons virgin olive oil
1 garlic clove, crushed
4 spring onions, shredded
 on the diagonal
450g orzo pasta
1 small butternut squash, peeled,
 deseeded and cut into 1cm
 cubes
1 litre well-flavoured chicken
 or vegetable stock
12 shiitake mushrooms,
 thickly sliced
15g unsalted butter
2 tablespoons grated pecorino
 cheese
1 jalapeño chilli, deseeded
 and finely chopped
1 tablespoon chopped mint
salt and freshly ground black
 pepper

Heat the olive oil in a heavy based pan, add the garlic and spring onions and cook for 1 minute.

Add the orzo and cook for a further minute, stirring to coat the pasta with the oil and garlic. Stir in the squash and cook for 5 minutes. Meanwhile, bring the stock to the boil in a separate pan and keep at simmering point.

Add the stock to the orzo a little at a time, stirring occasionally and making sure the pasta is always just covered by the liquid. After 10 minutes, add the mushrooms, then continue adding the stock until the orzo is *al dente*. Remove the pan from the heat, stir in the butter and season to taste.

Mix together the cheese, chilli and mint, scatter on top of the pasta and serve immediately.

Portabello mushrooms have a rich meaty flavour greatly prized in Italy and North America.

roasted portabello penne

with artichoke sauce

350g portabello mushrooms,
  cut into slices 5mm thick
12 garlic cloves, peeled
2 tablespoons olive oil
salt and freshly ground black
  pepper
450g penne pasta
25g unsalted butter
2 tablespoons freshly grated
  Parmesan cheese

for the sauce
4 cooked artichoke bottoms
1 tablespoon freshly grated
  Parmesan cheese
6 tablespoons olive oil
1 garlic clove, chopped
salt and freshly ground black
  pepper

Preheat the oven to 190°C/375°F/gas mark 5. Put the portabello mushrooms in a roasting tin with the garlic cloves, pour over the olive oil and season with salt and pepper. Roast for 15–20 minutes, until the mushrooms are tender and the garlic is caramelised.

Meanwhile, make the sauce. Put the artichokes, cheese, 2 tablespoons of the oil and the garlic in a blender and blitz to a purée. Then blend in the rest of the oil and season with salt and pepper.

Cook the penne in plenty of boiling salted water until *al dente*, then drain well. Return to the pan, add the butter and then add the artichoke sauce. Toss with the pasta. Season to taste, then transfer to a serving bowl and top with the roasted portabellos and garlic. Finally sprinkle over the Parmesan and serve.

PG TIPS
For a real treat, you could substitute wild mushrooms for the portabello mushrooms.

This dish is based on *fideau*, a classic paella from Valencia made with noodles instead of rice. Here I've used lumachine (little snails) pasta.

paprika pasta paella

900ml vegetable or chicken stock
½ teaspoon saffron strands
4 tablespoons olive oil
1 onion, finely chopped
1 teaspoon dried red chilli flakes
1 garlic clove, crushed
1 tablespoon hot Hungarian paprika
1 aubergine, cut into 1cm dice
1 red pepper, cut into 1cm dice
2 prepared artichoke hearts
400g can chopped tomatoes
450g lumachine pasta
50g French beans, cooked
salt and freshly ground black pepper

Put the stock and saffron in a pan and bring to the boil, then remove from the heat and set aside.

Heat the oil in a separate pan, add the onion, chilli flakes and garlic and fry over a moderate heat for 5 minutes, until golden. Stir in the paprika. Add the aubergine, red pepper and artichokes and stir to coat with the paprika, then add the tomatoes. Lower the heat and cook for 5–8 minutes.

Add the hot stock and bring to the boil, then add the pasta and spread it out evenly. Season with salt and pepper, reduce the heat and cook for 12–15 minutes. Taste the noodles to check they are cooked, then remove from the heat and allow to rest for a few minutes before serving.

spaghetti with lobster, basil & tomatoes

1 x 900g lobster, cooked
450g firm plum tomatoes,
 skinned, deseeded and cut into
 5mm dice
1 garlic clove, crushed
juice of ½ lemon
100ml lobster oil (see PG TIPS),
 made with the lobster shell
16 large basil leaves
450g spaghetti
salt and freshly ground black
 pepper
freshly grated Parmesan cheese
 to serve

Remove the lobster meat from the claws and body, cut it into chunks and set aside. Use the shell to make the lobster oil (see PG TIPS).

The following day, place the tomatoes, garlic, lemon juice and lobster oil in a bowl. Tear half the basil into small pieces and add to the bowl, then add the lobster chunks and season to taste. Leave to marinate at room temperature for up to 1 hour.

Cook the spaghetti in plenty of boiling salted water until *al dente*. Drain in a colander and return to the pan. Add the lobster and marinade and toss together. Place in a serving bowl and sprinkle over the Parmesan and the remaining torn basil leaves.

PG TIPS

To make lobster oil, crush the lobster shells into small pieces using a rolling pin and fry in 2 tablespoons oil for 10–15 minutes. Add a handful of chopped garlic, onion, celery and carrot, plus a bay leaf and a few tarragon stalks. Pour over 150ml dry white wine and simmer for 15 minutes. Reduce the heat, add 600ml vegetable oil and simmer for 30 minutes. Remove from the heat, cover and leave overnight (do not refrigerate). Strain through muslin or a filter and store in the fridge.

Pumpkin seeds are full of flavour and very nutritious. You can find them in health food stores but they are generally becoming more available everywhere. They give a wonderful nuttiness to the sauce in this unusual pasta dish.

linguine with pumpkin & mint sauce

& feta cheese

for the pumpkin seed mint sauce
150g pumpkin seeds
50g mint leaves
3 garlic cloves, chopped
a pinch of ground cumin
¼ teaspoon dried chilli flakes
150ml virgin olive oil

250g pumpkin flesh, cut into 1cm dice
4 tablespoons olive oil
salt and freshly ground black pepper
450g linguine
100g feta cheese, crumbled
shavings of Parmesan cheese to serve

Preheat the oven to 180°C/350°F/gas mark 4. For the sauce, roast the pumpkin seeds on a baking sheet for 10 minutes, until fragrant. Leave to cool, then place in a blender with the mint, garlic, cumin and chilli flakes. Blitz to a fine paste and then, with the motor running, slowly pour in enough olive oil to give a smooth, slightly runny sauce. Season and set aside.

Place the pumpkin on a baking sheet, toss with the olive oil and some salt and pepper and bake for 10–15 minutes, until tender and lightly browned. Meanwhile, cook the pasta in a large pan of boiling salted water until *al dente*. Drain the pasta, toss it with the sauce and adjust the seasoning. Top with the roasted pumpkin and feta cheese, sprinkle over some Parmesan shavings and serve.

Cooking the spaghetti in saffron water gives this dish
an unbelievable colour as well as taste.

saffron-cooked spaghetti

with baby spinach & fennel

1 quantity pasta dough (see
    page 6) or 400g dried spaghetti
4 tablespoons extra virgin olive oil
1 head of fennel, finely sliced,
    fronds removed and reserved
1 onion, thinly sliced
200g baby spinach leaves
5 tablespoons balsamic vinegar
2 good pinches of fresh saffron
75g pecorino romano cheese,
    grated
salt, freshly ground black pepper
    and ground nutmeg

Make the pasta dough into spaghetti (see page 6). Heat
half the oil in a large frying pan. Add the fennel slices
and onion and sauté over a moderate heat for 8–9
minutes or until soft and golden. Add the spinach and
cook until it wilts, then add the balsamic vinegar.

Bring 1 litre water to the boil in a large pan, add the
saffron and leave to simmer for 5 minutes for the
saffron to infuse the water. Cook the spaghetti in the
saffron water for 2–3 minutes or until *al dente*. Drain
well, reserving 120ml cooking water. Add the reserved
water to the vegetables and cook for 2–3 minutes. Add
the spaghetti, half the pecorino, toss well and season
with salt, freshly ground black pepper and nutmeg.

Place in 4 individual pasta bowls, top with the
remaining pecorino, garnish with the reserved fennel
fronds and serve immediately.

trenette frittata

with pepperone & clams

30 small venus clams
125ml dry white wine
6 tablespoons olive oil
3 garlic cloves, crushed
1 red pepper, cut into 5mm dice
½ teaspoon dried red chilli flakes
75g pepperone, cut into 2.5cm slices
250g trenette (or linguine)
5 large eggs, lightly beaten
1 tablespoon chopped flat leaf
   parsley
salt and freshly ground black pepper

Scrub the clams under cold running water, discarding any open ones that don't close when tapped on a work surface. Put them in a large pan, pour over the white wine, then cover and place on a high heat for 1–2 minutes, until the clams open. Drain in a colander, then strain the juices through a fine sieve and reserve. Shell the clams and set aside.

Heat 3 tablespoons of the olive oil in a small frying pan, add the garlic and cook over a low heat until softened. Add the red pepper, dried chilli flakes and pepperone slices and cook until the pepper is softened. Then add the clams and their juice and cook for 1 minute. Remove the pan from the heat and set aside.

Cook the pasta in plenty of boiling salted water until *al dente*, then drain well. In a bowl, toss the pasta with the clam and pepper mixture and leave to cool. Add the beaten eggs and the parsley to the cooled pasta mixture and season with salt and pepper.

Heat the remaining oil in a small frying pan. Add the pasta mixture and spread it out with a fork. Reduce the heat and, stirring carefully from time to time, cook until browned underneath and just set. Place a large plate over the pan and invert the frittata on to it. Slide the frittata, browned-side up, back into the pan and cook for 2 more minutes. Turn out on to a serving plate and leave to cool slightly before cutting into wedges to serve.

oodles of noodles

The word 'noodle' possibly comes from the German word '*Nudel*' meaning 'pasta'. The recipes in this chapter include Spanish *fideos* noodles, and Austrian *spaetzle*, noodle-cum-dumplings, but predominantly feature Asian products and flavours. Asian noodles are made from numerous varieties of flour, most commonly wheat flour, rice flour, potato flour, even mung bean flour. They consist of strands that vary in shape, width and length, symbolizing longevity. They can also be found as thin sticks, flat strands, round strands and wavy lines. Asian noodles are available dried or fresh and are eaten hot or cold, used in soups, salads, stir fries and other Asian dishes.

egg noodles

These are made from eggs and wheat, most commonly dried in bundles, and are best used in stir fries and soups. Boil them for a few seconds before adding to any dish.

rice noodles

Popular in southern China, white in colour, these come in a variety of shapes, most commonly rice stick noodles. Soak in warm water for 15 minutes, then drain well. Use in soups, salads and stir fries.

cellophane noodles

Also called glass or transparent noodles, these are made from mung bean starch.

Soak for 10 minutes before cooking. These noodles are packed in plastic wrapped bundles. They are usually added to soups and braised Chinese dishes, and often deep fried until crispy and used as a garnish.

ramen noodles

These fresh Japanese-style noodles are made from wheat flour, egg and water. Boil for 2–3 minutes, then add to hot noodle soups, or mix with a sauce in stir fries.

soba noodles

These slightly chewy Japanese noodles are made from buckwheat and plain flour, available dried or fresh. Add to noodle soups, salads and cold dishes.

udon noodles

Made from wheat flour, these white noodles come in round or flat varieties. Cook in boiling water before adding them to Japanese miso style soups and braised dishes with a sauce.

Hokkien noodles

Also known as Singapore noodles, these thick, yellowy, somewhat chewy noodles are again made from wheat flour. They are purchased cooked and lightly oiled and need no preparation. Simply add to stir fries, soups and salads.

thai stir-fried noodles

225g dried rice noodles
2 red chillies, deseeded and finely
  chopped
2 shallots, sliced
3 tablespoons *nam pla* (Thai fish
  sauce)
2 tablespoons brown sugar
2 tablespoons tamarind paste
1 teaspoon lime juice
4 tablespoons vegetable oil
125g pork fillet, cut into small,
  thin strips
150g fresh shrimps, peeled
50g shiitake mushrooms, sliced
75g beansprouts
2 tablespoons *ketjap manis*
  (Indonesian soy sauce)
salt and freshly ground black pepper

Soak the noodles in a bowl of warm water for about
10 minutes, until softened, then drain in a colander.

Place the chillies, shallots, fish sauce and sugar in
a mortar and crush to a paste. Add the tamarind
and lime juice and pound until smooth. Mix in
2 tablespoons of water and set aside.

Heat the oil in a wok until very hot, add the spice paste
and stir fry for 1 minute. Add the pork and shrimps,
mix well with the paste and cook for 2–3 minutes. Add
the noodles, mushrooms, beansprouts and soy sauce
and season with salt and pepper. Stir fry for 2 minutes
and then serve immediately.

Austrian noodles

with Savoy cabbage, mushrooms & chestnuts

for the *spaetzle noodles*
275g plain flour
100g buckwheat flour
salt and freshly ground black
   pepper
6 free-range eggs, beaten
iced water

25g unsalted butter
1 tablespoon mild olive oil
1 shallot, finely chopped
1 garlic clove, crushed
200g chanterelle mushrooms,
   cleaned
1 tablespoon chopped fresh
   flat leaf parsley
75g vacuum-packed chestnuts
150g Savoy cabbage or *cavolo nero*,
   finely shredded
100ml double cream
1 tablespoon grated Gruyère or
   Emmental
1 tablespoon truffle oil

For the *spaetzle* noodles, sift both flours and a little salt into a large bowl. Make a well in the centre, tip in the beaten eggs and mix them into the flour with enough water to form a thick but runny batter.

Bring a large pan of salted water to the boil and place a large-holed colander over it (ensuring the colander does not touch the water). Pour in a little of the batter at a time and push through the colander with a spatula into the water. When the noodles rise to the surface – after about 1 minute – remove them with a slotted spoon into iced water. Drain well in another colander and dry in a cloth.

For the vegetables, heat the butter and oil in a large frying pan over a gentle heat, add the shallot and garlic and cook until tender. Raise the heat, add the chanterelles, parsley and chestnuts and fry until golden. Add the cabbage or *cavolo nero*, toss together, add 100ml water and cook for 3–4 minutes.

Throw in the *spaetzle*, toss with the vegetables and heat through. Add the cream and cheese and season to taste. Place in a serving dish, drizzle over the truffle oil and serve.

red pepper noodles

with melting Gruyère

2 red peppers
1 large red chilli
4 tablespoons olive oil
175g plain flour
¼ teaspoon baking powder
2 free-range eggs
salt and freshly ground black
  pepper
freshly grated nutmeg
50g Gruyère cheese, grated

Preheat the oven to 180°C/350°F/gas mark 4. Place the peppers and chilli in a baking dish, spoon over 2 tablespoons of the oil and roast for 40 minutes, until soft and lightly charred. Remove from the oven and place in a bowl, cover with clingfilm and leave for 5 minutes. Peel and deseed, then place in a blender and blitz to a purée.

Sift the flour and baking powder into a bowl. Beat in the eggs, then add the red pepper purée. Season with salt, pepper and nutmeg.

Bring a large pan of salted water to the boil. Rest a colander over the pan. Pour a little of the batter into the colander and press through the holes using a spatula. When the *spaetzle* noodles float to the surface, cover the pan until they are swollen and fluffy, about 3–4 minutes. Remove the *spaetzle* with a slotted spoon and dunk into iced water to refresh them. Drain well, then leave to dry on a cloth.

To serve, heat the remaining oil in a large frying pan, add the *spaetzle* noodles and toss them in the oil until heated through and lightly golden. Season with salt, pepper and nutmeg and transfer to a serving dish. Sprinkle over the Gruyère and place under a hot grill until the cheese begins to melt. Serve immediately.

This vegetarian stir-fried rice noodle dish is one of countless Thai variations on a theme, both interesting and tasty, and the tofu provides valuable soya protein. Pickled white radish is available in tins and can be sourced from Asian grocers.

Pad tofu

300g vermicelli rice noodles
1 tablespoon peanut
  (groundnut) oil
2 garlic cloves, crushed
½ tablespoon finely chopped
  fresh root ginger
1 red chilli, thinly sliced
300g Chinese broccoli, trimmed
  and chopped into pieces
100g beansprouts
2 tablespoons chopped pickled
  white radish
1 tablespoon brown sugar
20ml soy sauce
1 tablespoon sweet chilli sauce
4 spring onions, shredded
175g firm tofu
2 tablespoons roughly chopped
  coriander leaves
2 tablespoons chopped
  roasted peanuts
freshly ground black pepper

Place the rice noodles in a bowl, cover with boiling water, leave to soften and then drain them well.

In a wok or large non-stick frying pan, heat the peanut oil, add the garlic, ginger and chilli and stir fry for 1 minute.

Add the broccoli, beansprouts and radish and cook for a further minute. Add the sugar, soy and chilli sauces and toss well together.

Throw in the spring onions, tofu, coriander and peanuts. Season with black pepper to taste and serve in bowls.

wok-fried noodles

with dried spiced beef

350g beef skirt
1 tablespoon crushed garlic
1 tablespoon palm sugar
2 red Thai chillies, deseeded and
  finely chopped
2.5cm piece of fresh galangal
  (or root ginger), peeled and
  finely sliced
2 teaspoons *blachan* (dried
  shrimp paste)
½ teaspoon ground cloves
2 tablespoons vegetable oil
salt and freshly ground black
  pepper
450g egg thread noodles

Bring 2 litres of water to the boil, add the beef and poach for 1 hour or until it is so tender that the meat fibres separate easily. Leave to cool a little and then shred it finely with a fork.

Put the garlic, palm sugar, chillies, galangal, shrimp paste and ground cloves in a blender or food processor and blitz to a coarse paste. Heat the oil in a frying pan and cook the paste over a moderate heat for 2–3 minutes, until fragrant. Add the shredded beef, mix well and sauté until the moisture from the spice paste has evaporated and the meat is tacky. Season to taste.

Place the noodles in a bowl, pour over plenty of boiling salted water and leave for 30 seconds to swell. Drain them well, toss with the spiced beef and serve immediately.

fried ginger noodles

with *pak choi* & spring onions

450g egg thread noodles
2 tablespoons vegetable oil
2.5cm piece of fresh root ginger,
   finely chopped
1 garlic clove, crushed
4 *pak choi*, separated into leaves
2 tablespoons oyster sauce
1 tablespoon dark soy sauce
1 teaspoon *nam pla*
   (Thai fish sauce)
4 spring onions, finely shredded

Place the noodles in a large bowl and pour over enough boiling water to cover. Leave for 30 seconds, then drain in a colander.

Heat the vegetable oil in a wok or a large frying pan, add the ginger and garlic, then add the *pak choi* leaves and stir fry for 1 minute. Add the drained noodles, oyster sauce, soy and fish sauces and mix well together.

Serve immediately, sprinkled with the shredded spring onions.

potato noodles

with prawns in their own sauce

for the noodles
400g floury potatoes
50g Parmesan cheese,
  freshly grated
150g plain flour
salt and freshly ground
  black pepper
2 eggs, lightly beaten
50g unsalted butter, melted
chervil leaves, to garnish

for the prawns
4 tablespoons olive oil
20 raw tiger prawns, peeled and
  deveined – reserve the heads
  and shells
100g finely chopped mixed carrot,
  leek and onion
2 tablespoons brandy
100ml dry white wine
1 tablespoon tomato purée
150ml double cream
25g chilled unsalted butter, cut
  into small pieces

Preheat the oven to 200°C/400°F/gas mark 6. Wrap each potato in foil and bake until tender, then peel. Pass the potato flesh through a sieve into a large bowl. Mix in the Parmesan, flour and some salt and pepper. Make a well in the centre, pour in the eggs and bring together to form a dough. Knead the dough for 1–2 minutes, then wrap in clingfilm and leave to rest for 30 minutes.

Shape the dough into a long roll about 2.5cm in diameter and cut it into 1cm slices. Roll each one under your hand on a floured surface until it is a 5cm long torpedo shape. Set aside on a floured baking tray.

Heat the oil in a large pan, add the prawn heads and shells and sauté for 2–3 minutes. Add the chopped vegetables and cook for 4–5 minutes. Pour in the brandy and wine and boil for 5 minutes, then stir in the tomato purée. Pour over enough water to cover the shells, bring to the boil, then reduce the heat, add the cream and simmer for 10 minutes. Pulverise briefly in a blender, then strain through a fine sieve into a clean pan. Poach the prawns for 2 minutes in the sauce, until cooked. Whisk in the butter and season to taste. Keep warm.

Poach the noodles in boiling salted water for 2–3 minutes until they rise to the surface. Remove with a slotted spoon, toss with the melted butter and season to taste. Arrange on serving plates and pour over the prawns in their own sauce. Garnish with chervil leaves.

A *fideau* is a Spanish noodle dish. In this recipe, a collection of wild and cultivated mushrooms cooked in an enriched mushroom stock form the base of the dish.

black mushroom spanish noodles

for the stock
450g flat mushrooms
2 teaspoons tomato purée
2 tablespoons mild olive oil
1 onion, chopped
1 garlic clove, crushed
few coriander stalks
1.5 litres vegetable stock

2 tablespoons olive oil
1 onion, finely chopped
1 garlic clove, crushed
700g wild and cultivated
   mushrooms (i.e. chestnut,
   trompettes, girolles, shiitake),
   cleaned and cut into pieces
½ teaspoon smoked paprika
180g fideos noodles (or spaghetti)
120g orzo pasta
4 tomatoes, blanched, skinned and
   chopped
150ml aïoli (garlic mayonnaise)
   (see PG TIPS)

For the base stock, place the flat mushrooms and tomato purée in a food processor and blend to a coarse mush. Heat the olive oil in a pan, add the onion and garlic and cook for 2–3 minutes. Add the mushroom tomato mixture and coriander stalks and cook over a high heat for 5 minutes, stirring regularly. Add the vegetable stock and simmer for a further 15 minutes. Strain the stock through a fine strainer and keep hot.

Preheat the oven to 180°C/350°F/gas mark 4. Heat the olive oil in a casserole dish, add the onions and garlic and cook for 1 minute. Throw in the mushrooms and smoked paprika and cook over a high heat for 2 minutes. Pour over the hot mushroom stock and bring to the boil. Stir in noodles and pasta and the tomatoes, reduce the heat to a simmer and cook for 6 minutes. Place in the oven for 5–6 minutes to finish cooking and lightly crisp the surface. Leave to cool slightly. Serve with the aïoli.

PG TIPS
For the aïoli, crush 2 garlic cloves in a mortar. Mix in 1 egg yolk. Trickle in 150ml olive oil, stirring constantly to mix thoroughly. Add salt and a dash of lemon juice.

My Asian variety of the classic Italian pesto sauce uses mint and coriander spiced with ginger and is great for a salad dressing or served with grilled fish.

shiitake mushroom noodles

with Asian pesto

for the pesto
40g mint leaves
40g coriander leaves
1 garlic clove, crushed
25g roasted peanuts
2.5cm piece root ginger, peeled and finely chopped
1 tablespoon olive oil
pinch of sugar

400g Chinese egg noodles
1 tablespoon sesame oil
125g shiitake mushrooms, thickly sliced
1 garlic clove, crushed
1cm piece of fresh root ginger, peeled and finely chopped
1 green chilli, deseeded and thinly sliced
4 spring onions, shredded
40ml soy sauce

To make the pesto, place all the ingredients in a blender, blitz to a coarse purée and set aside.

Soak the noodles for 3–4 minutes in a bowl of boiling water, then drain them well.

In a large non-stick pan or wok, heat the sesame oil until very hot, then add the sliced shiitake mushrooms and sauté for 1 minute or until they are slightly softened. Add the garlic, ginger and chilli and continue to stir fry. Add the spring onions and soy sauce and toss together.

Add the drained noodles and the pesto, toss together until heated through and serve.

A simple and quick dish to prepare when you are hungry and short of time. The flavours from the Far East and Italy blend well together; remember, it was Marco Polo who allegedly introduced pasta to the Western world, bringing it back from China.

my fusion noodles

400g Chinese egg noodles
2 tablespoons olive oil
½ garlic clove, crushed
1 red chilli, deseeded and finely chopped
2.5cm piece of root ginger, peeled and chopped
175g shiitake mushrooms, thinly sliced
3 tablespoons pesto sauce (see page 18)

Bring a large pan of water to the boil, add the noodles and cook according to the packet instructions. Drain in a colander and set aside.

Heat the oil in a large frying pan, add the garlic, chilli and ginger and cook for 1 minute. Throw in the shiitake mushrooms and cook for a further 2–3 minutes.

Add the cooked noodles and toss with the mushrooms, using a pair of kitchen tongs. Finally, add the pesto sauce and toss again. Place in 4 serving bowls and serve immediately.

chilli crab noodle omelette

150g fresh rice noodles
8 organic or free-range eggs
2 teaspoons *nam pla* (Thai fish
  sauce)
1 red chilli, deseeded and finely
  chopped
1 tablespoon chopped coriander
salt and freshly ground black pepper
oil, for frying
4 spring onions, shredded
  on the diagonal
150g fresh crabmeat

Cook the rice noodles in a large pan of boiling water for about 5 minutes, until tender, then drain well and dry. Set aside.

Beat the eggs in a bowl with the fish sauce, chilli, half the coriander and some salt and pepper.

Heat 2 tablespoons of oil in a frying pan, add the spring onions and cook for 1 minute. Add the crab and warm through, then season to taste. Keep warm.

Heat a little oil in an omelette pan, add a quarter of the noodles and toss for 30 seconds to reheat them. Pour in a quarter of the beaten egg mixture and cook, drawing in the egg mixture from the sides of the pan, until set underneath. Spoon a quarter of the crab mixture down the centre of the omelette, fold in half and turn out on to a warm plate and keep warm while you cook the remaining 3 omelettes in the same way. Serve immediately, sprinkled with a little of the remaining coriander.

One of my favourite memories during my short time working in Singapore is eating this simple Asian vegetable dish of crunchy cooked vegetables, on top of a bed of crispy rice noodles.

mee krob

groundnut or vegetable oil for deep-frying
125g rice vermicelli noodles
2 tablespoons vegetable oil
6 shallots, finely sliced
3 garlic cloves, crushed
1 red chilli, very thinly sliced
100g firm tofu, cut into 1cm dice (optional)
50g peanuts, chopped
1 small butternut squash, peeled and thinly sliced
100g oyster mushrooms, cut into strips
4 large spring onions, sliced thinly
100g baby sweetcorn
75g French beans, topped, tailed and blanched
75g beansprouts
2 tablespoons palm sugar (or brown sugar)
2 tablespoons rice wine vinegar (or white wine vinegar)
1 teaspoon vegetarian fish sauce (*nuoc mam chay*) – optional
juice of 1 lime
50g fresh coriander leaves

Heat the oil in a frying pan or large pan. When the oil is hot add the noodles, a few at a time, until puffed up and cooked – only a matter of seconds. Remove with a slotted spoon on to kitchen paper and drain thoroughly.

Heat a wok or large frying pan with 2 tablespoons of vegetable oil, add the shallots and garlic and cook until they turn golden. Add the chilli, tofu (if using), peanuts and vegetables and stir fry for 2–3 minutes. Add the palm sugar, vinegar, fish sauce and lime juice and cook for a further 30 seconds. Divide the fried noodles between 4 serving plates, top with the vegetables, garnish with the coriander leaves and serve.

Most supermarkets sell cooked seafood, which is pretty good quality and certainly takes a lot of tedious preparation work out of this dish. This is a simple but satisfying salad, perfect for the summer months.

chilled noodle seafood salad

for the dressing
½ teaspoon Dijon mustard
½ garlic clove, crushed
juice of 1 lemon
1 tablespoon olive oil
1 teaspoon honey

250g dried rice noodles or tagliatelle
250g pack cooked seafood selection
4 spring onions, shredded
2 plum tomatoes, deseeded and
  chopped
¼ cucumber, chopped
freshly ground black pepper
2 tablespoons roughly chopped dill

First make the dressing by placing the mustard and garlic in a large bowl. Add the lemon juice, olive oil and honey, whisking well to amalgamate.

Cook the noodles in boiling water until tender, drain well, then add to the dressing and toss thoroughly together. (Adding the noodles when hot allows them to absorb the flavours in the dressing.) Add the seafood, spring onions, chopped tomatoes and cucumber, season with black pepper to taste and leave to cool to room temperature.

Add the dill and toss before serving.

spicy vegetable & cashew ramen

4 tablespoons vegetable oil
100g sugar snap peas
2 red peppers, seeded, cut into strips lengthways
4 small aubergines, cut into thin slices
350g shiitake mushrooms
2 garlic cloves, crushed
1 small red chilli, deseeded, finely chopped
2.5cm piece root ginger
2 tablespoons light soy sauce
1 teaspoon light brown sugar
½ litre light chicken or vegetable stock
450g wholemeal ramen noodles
75g cashew nuts (or peanuts)
2 tablespoons freshly chopped coriander

Heat the vegetable oil in a wok or large frying pan, add the vegetables, garlic, chilli and ginger and stir fry for 4–5 minutes.

Add the soy sauce, sugar and stock and simmer for a further 5 minutes.

Cook the noodles in a large pan of boiling water for 2–3 minutes or until just tender. Drain them well.

Divide the noodles between 4 serving bowls, then pour over the vegetables and some of the chicken broth. Scatter over the cashew nuts, add the chopped coriander, then serve.

index